BOOK TWO

HAL LEONARD
GUITAR
TAB METHOD
SONGBOOK

ISBN 978-1-4768-1205-2

HAL•LEONARD®
CORPORATION

7777 W. BLUEMOUND RD. P.O. BOX 13819 MILWAUKEE, WI 53213

Visit Hal Leonard Online at
www.halleonard.com

TABLE OF CONTENTS

Mr. Jones

Words by Adam Duritz
Music by Adam Duritz and David Bryson

Key of C
Intro
Moderately fast

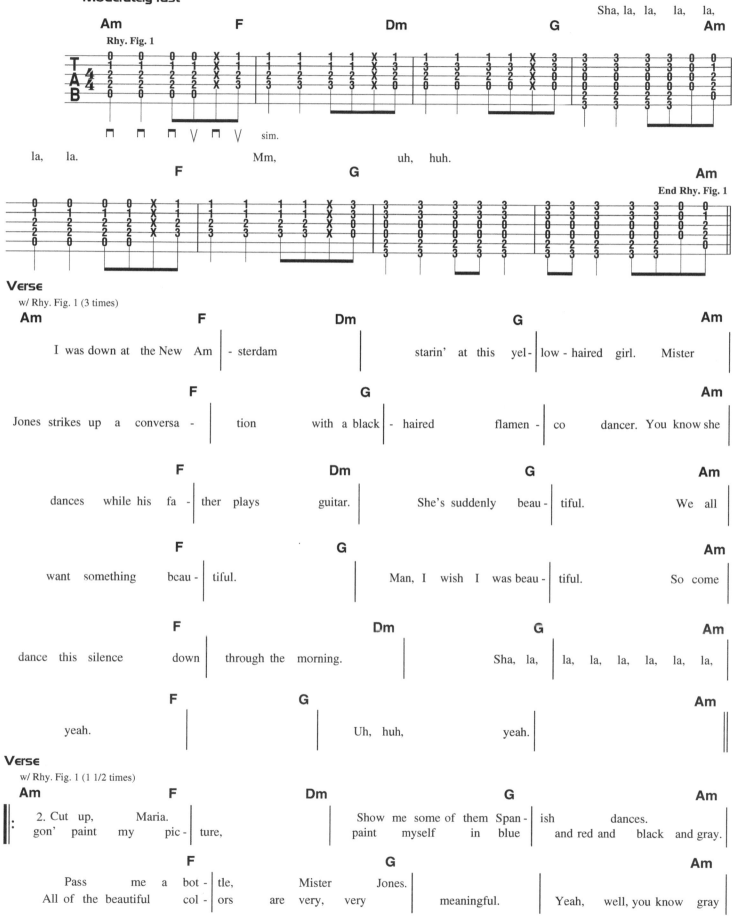

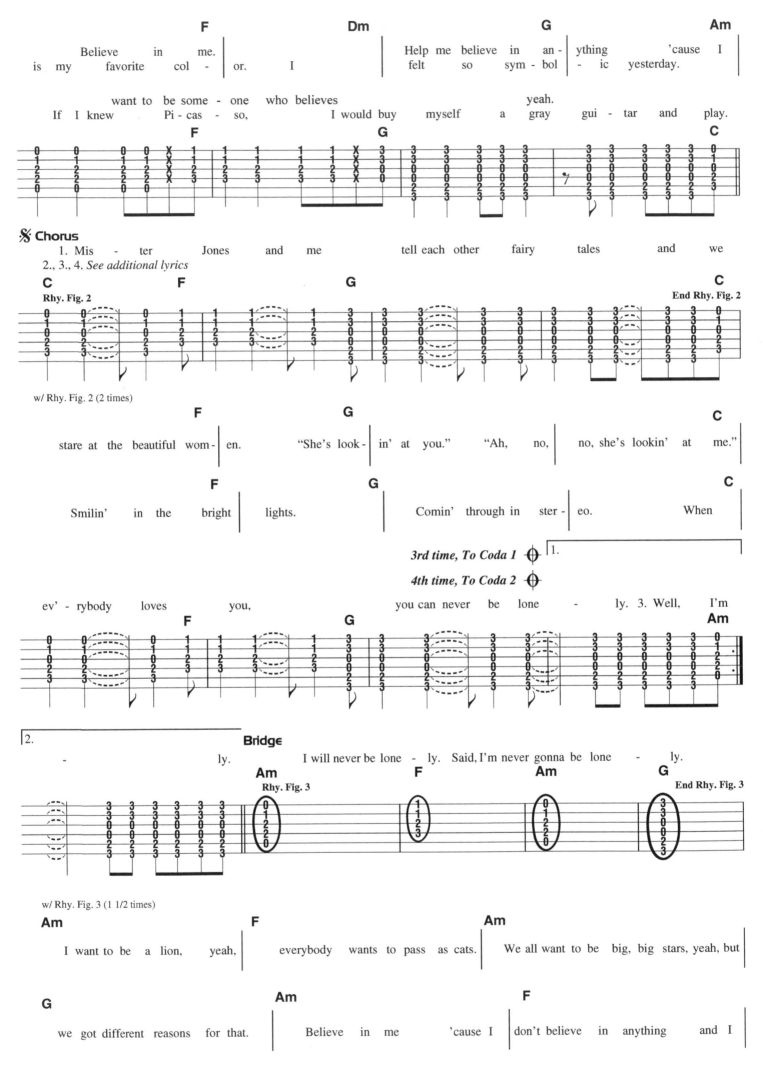

F **Dm** **G** **Am**

Believe in me. Help me believe in an- | ything 'cause I
is my favorite col - | or. I felt so sym - bol | - ic yesterday.

want to be some - one who believes yeah.
If I knew Pi - cas - so, I would buy myself a gray gui - tar and play.

F **G** **C**

𝄋 Chorus

1. Mis - ter Jones and me tell each other fairy tales and we
2., 3., 4. *See additional lyrics*

C **F** **G** **C**

Rhy. Fig. 2 End Rhy. Fig. 2

w/ Rhy. Fig. 2 (2 times)

F **G** **C**

stare at the beautiful wom - | en. "She's look - | in' at you." "Ah, no, | no, she's lookin' at me."

F **G** **C**

Smilin' in the bright | lights. Comin' through in ster - | eo. When

3rd time, To Coda 1 ⊕ | 1.

4th time, To Coda 2 ⊕

ev' - rybody loves you, you can never be lone - | ly. 3. Well, I'm

F **G** **Am**

| 2.

Bridge

- | ly. I will never be lone - | ly. Said, I'm never gonna be lone - | ly.

Am **F** **Am** **G**

Rhy. Fig. 3 End Rhy. Fig. 3

w/ Rhy. Fig. 3 (1 1/2 times)

Am **F** **Am**

I want to be a lion, yeah, | everybody wants to pass as cats. | We all want to be big, big stars, yeah, but

G **Am** **F**

we got different reasons for that. | Believe in me 'cause I | don't believe in anything and I

4

wanna be someone to believe, to believe, to believe, yeah.   - ky   as you   can be.

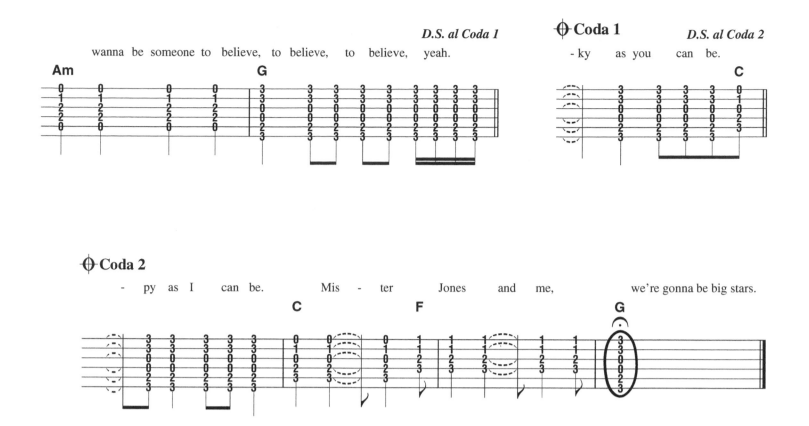

✛ Coda 2

- py   as   I   can be.   Mis - ter   Jones   and   me,   we're gonna be big stars.

Additional Lyrics

2. Mister Jones and me look into the future.
   Yeah, we stare at the beautiful women.
   "She's looking at you."
   "Uh, I don't think so, she's lookin' at me."
   Standin' in the spotlight.
   I bought myself a gray guitar.
   When everybody loves me, I will never be lonely.

3. Mister Jones and me stumblin' through the barrio.
   Yeah, we stare at the beautiful women.
   "She's perfect for you,
   Man, there's got to be somebody for me."
   I wanna be Bob Dylan.
   Mister Jones wishes he was someone just a little more funky.
   When everybody loves you,
   Ah, son, just about as funky as you can be.

4. Mister Jones and me starin' at the video.
   When I look at the television,
   I want to see me staring right back at me.
   We all want to be big stars,
   But we don't know why, and we don't know how.
   But when everybody loves me,
   I'm gonna be just about as happy as I can be.

Born Under a Bad Sign

Words and Music by Booker T. Jones and William Bell

Key of C#

Intro

Moderately slow

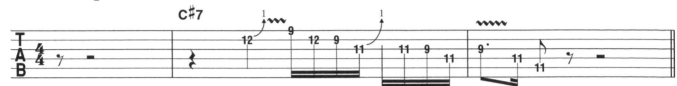

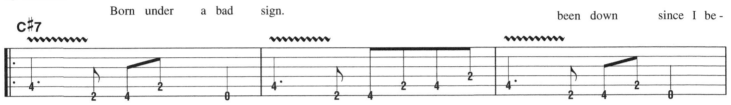

§ Chorus

Born under a bad sign.　　been down　　since I be-

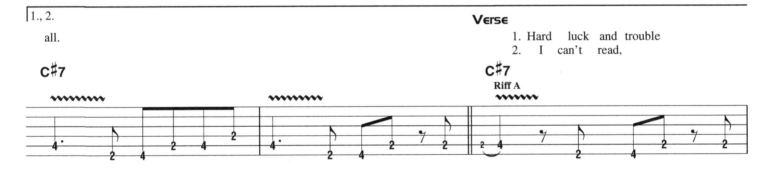

To Coda ✛

gan to crawl.　　If it wasn't for bad luck,　　you know I wouldn't have　　no luck at

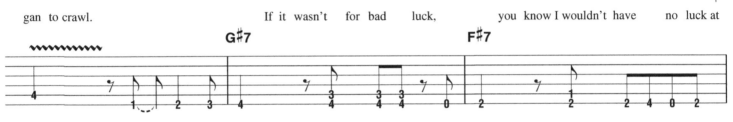

‖1., 2.　　　　　　　　　　　　　**Verse**

all.　　　　　　　　　　1. Hard luck and trouble
　　　　　　　　　　　　2. I can't read,

C#7　　　　　　　　　　　　　　C#7
　　　　　　　　　　　　　　Riff A

been my only friend.　　I been on my own　　ever since I was ten.
I haven't learned how to write.　My whole life has been　　one big fight.

End Riff A

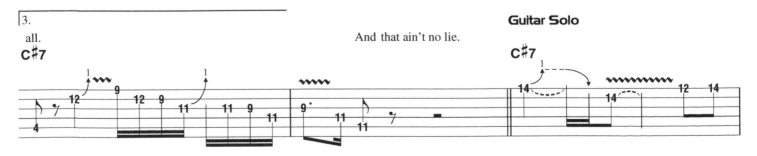

‖3.

all.　　　　　　　　And that ain't no lie.　　　**Guitar Solo**

C#7　　　　　　　　　　　　　　C#7

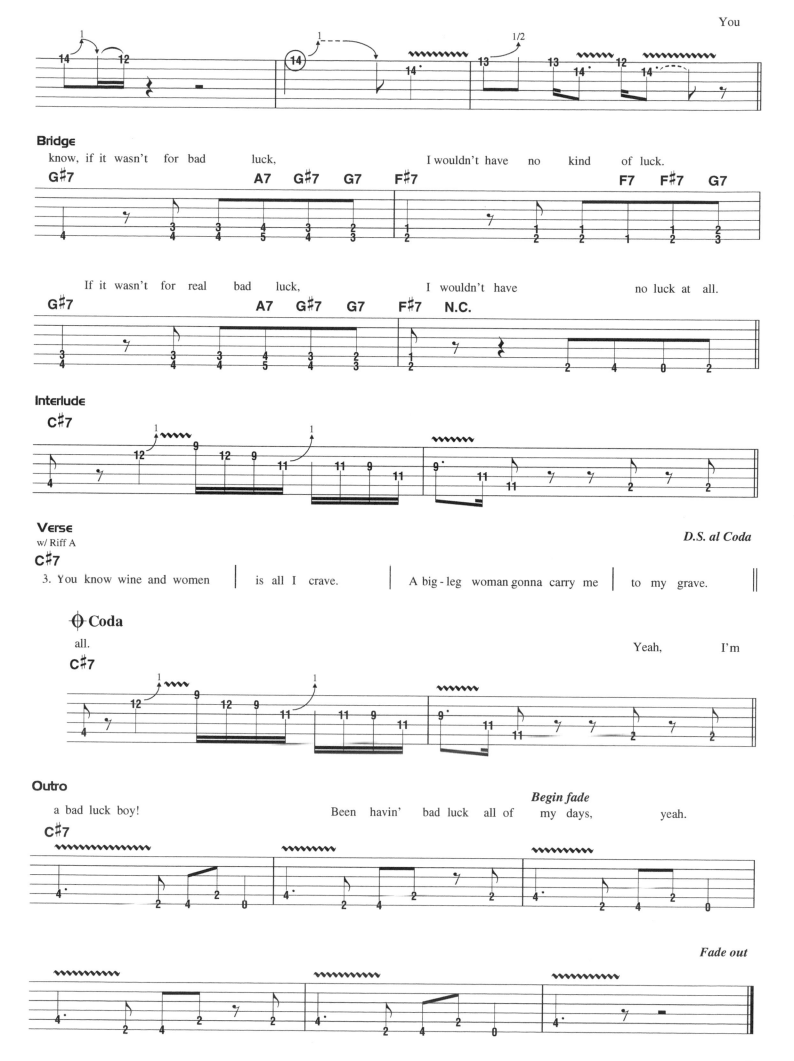

Bridge

know, if it wasn't for bad luck, I wouldn't have no kind of luck.

If it wasn't for real bad luck, I wouldn't have no luck at all.

Interlude

Verse
w/ Riff A

D.S. al Coda

3. You know wine and women is all I crave. A big-leg woman gonna carry me to my grave.

Coda

all. Yeah, I'm

Outro

a bad luck boy! *Begin fade* Been havin' bad luck all of my days, yeah.

Fade out

Brain Stew

Words by Billie Joe Armstrong
Music by Green Day

Key of Am

Intro
Moderately slow

A5　　　G5　　　F#5　　　F5　　E5

Rhy. Fig. 1 　　　　　　　　　　　　　　　End Rhy. Fig. 1

```
T  . ||--------------|--------------|--------------|--------------|--------------. ||
A 4 . ||-7--7----7----|-5--5----7----|-4--4----7----|-3-3----2-2----|--------------. ||
B 4 . ||-7--7---------|-5--5---------|-4--4---------|-3-3----2-2--7-|--------------. ||
   . ||-5--5---------|-3--3---------|-2--2---------|-1-1----0-0----|--------------. ||
```

Verse
w/ Rhy. Fig. 1 (4 times)

A5　　　　G5　　　　F#5　　　F5　　E5　　　A5　　　　G5

1. I'm having trouble try'n' to | sleep. | I'm countin' sheep but runnin' |

F#5　　　F5　　E5　　　A5　　　　G5　　　　F#5　　　F5　　E5

out. | As time ticks by, | still I try. |

Interlude
w/ Rhy. Fig. 1 (2 times)

A5　　　　G5　　　　F#5　　　F5　　E5　　　A5　　G5

No rest for crosstops in my | mind.   On my own, here we go. || | |

F#5　　　F5　　E5　　　A5　　　　G5　　　　F#5　　　F5　　E5

| | | |

Verse
w/ Rhy. Fig. 1 (3 times)

A5　　　　G5　　　　F#5　　　F5　E5　A5　　　　G5

|: 2. My eyes feel like they're gonna | bleed. | Dried up and bulging out my |
　3. My mind is set on over- | drive, | The clock is laughing in my |

F#5　　　F5　　E5　　　A5　　　　G5　　　　F#5　　　F5　　E5

skull. | My mouth is dry, | my face is numb. |
face. | A crooked spine, | my senses dulled. |

F**ked up and spun out in my room.   } On my own, here we go.
Past the point of delirium.

A5　　　　　　　　G5　　　　　　F#5　　　F5　　　E5

```
T ------------------|--------------|--------------|--------------|-----------||
A -7--7----7----4---|-5--5----7----|-4--4----7----|-3-3:----2-2:--|-----------||
B -7--7----4----4---|-5--5---------|-4--4---------|-3-3:----2-2:--|-----------||
  -5--5----4--------|-3--3---------|-2--2---------|-1-1:----0-0:--|-----------||
```

Interlude

*Natural harmonics occur while sliding fret hand up and down strings while executing muffled string strums.

Verse

w/ Rhy. Fig. 1 (3 times)

A5   G5   F#5   F5   E5

4. My   eyes   feel   like   they're   gonna   bleed.

A5   G5   F#5   F5   E5

Dried   up   and   bulging   out   my   skull.

A5   G5   F#5   F5   E5

My   mouth   is   dry,   my   face   is   numb.

F**ked   up   and   spun   out   in   my   room.   On   my   own,   here   we   go.

Outro

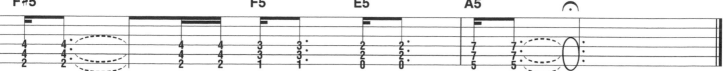

9

Fortunate Son

Words and Music by John Fogerty

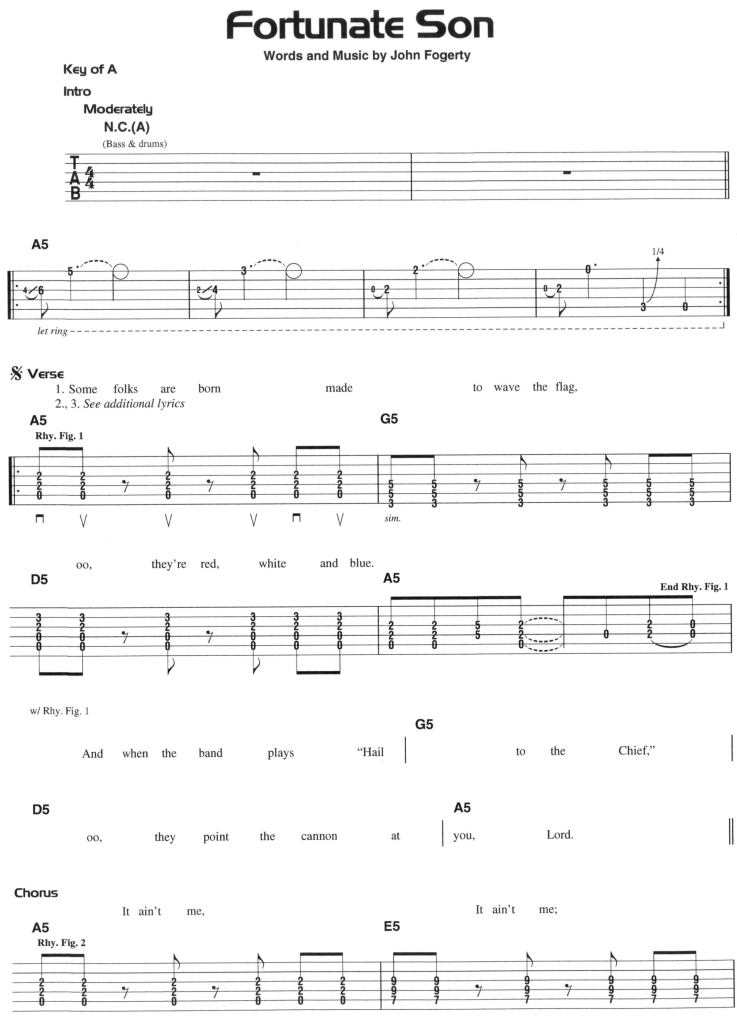

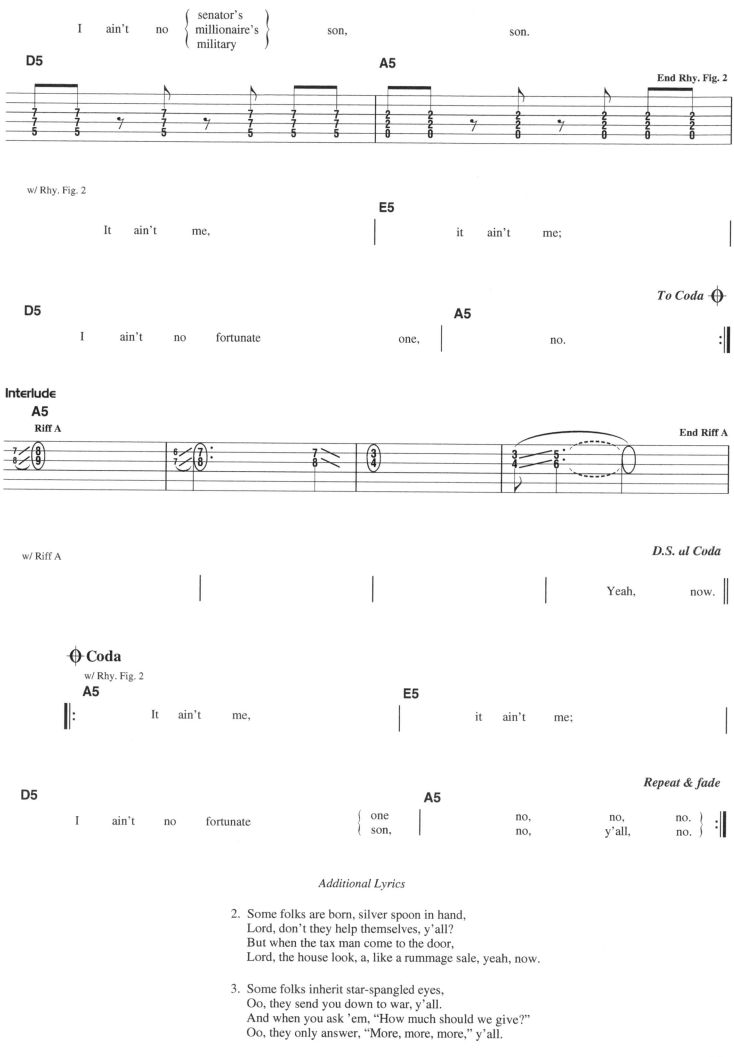

Additional Lyrics

2. Some folks are born, silver spoon in hand,
   Lord, don't they help themselves, y'all?
   But when the tax man come to the door,
   Lord, the house look, a, like a rummage sale, yeah, now.

3. Some folks inherit star-spangled eyes,
   Oo, they send you down to war, y'all.
   And when you ask 'em, "How much should we give?"
   Oo, they only answer, "More, more, more," y'all.

I Won't Back Down

Words and Music by Tom Petty and Jeff Lynne

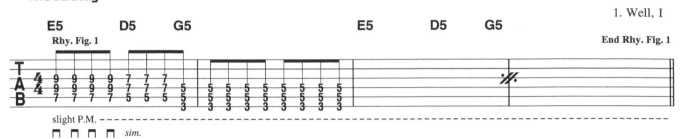

Key of G

Intro

Moderately

1. Well, I

End Rhy. Fig. 1

Verse

w/ Rhy. Fig. 1

E5	D5	G5			E5	D5	G5	
won't	back	down.		No, I	won't	back	down.	You can
stand	my	ground.		Won't be	turned	a -	round.	And I'll
know	what's	right.		I got	just	one	life	in a

stand me up at the gates of hell, but I won't back down.
keep this world from draggin' me down, gonna stand my ground,
world that keeps on pushin' me around. But I'll stand my ground,

[1.]

2. No, I'll

[2.]

and I won't back down. (I won't back down.)

E5 D5 G5 C5 G5 C5

Rhy. Fig. 2   End Rhy. Fig. 2

slight P.M.

Chorus

Hey, baby, there ain't no easy way out.

C5 G5 D5 G5 C5 G5 D5

Rhy. Fig. 3

slight P.M.

(I won't back down.) Hey, I will

G5 C5 G5 D5

End Rhy. Fig. 3

slight P.M.   slight P.M.

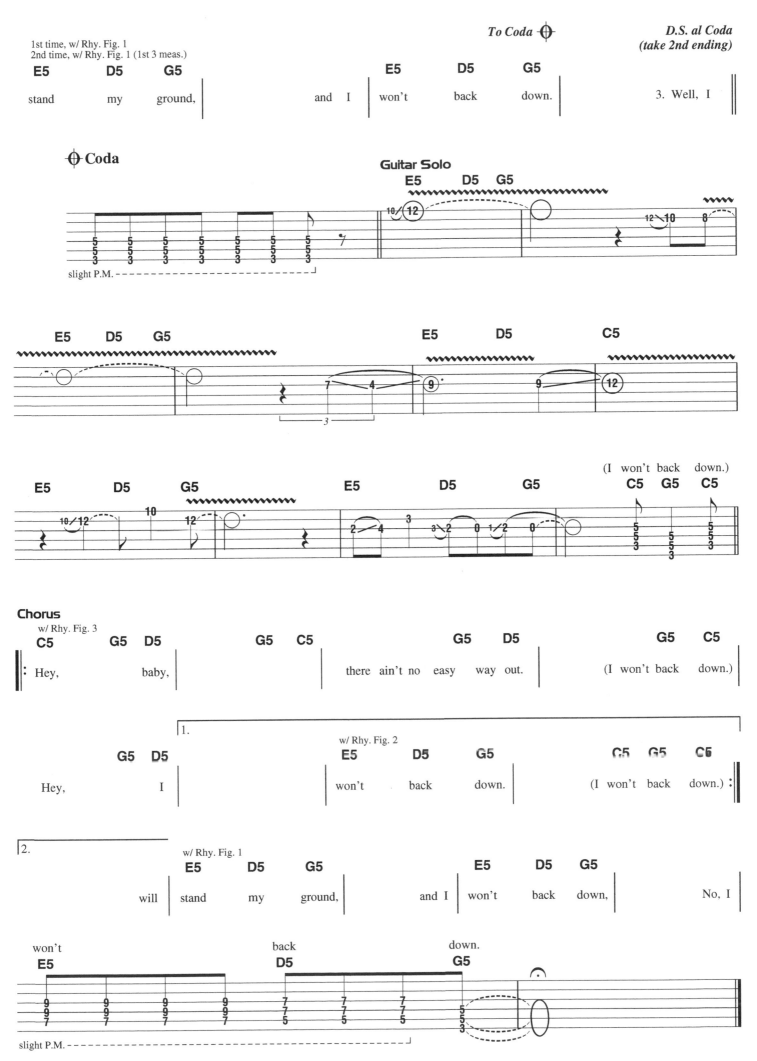

Lithium

Words and Music by Kurt Cobain

Key of E

Intro

Moderately

E5   G#5   C#5   A5

Rhy. Fig. 1

P.M. ---------   *let ring* ------   P.M.   *let ring* ------   P.M.   *let ring* ---------   P.M.

C5   D5   B5   D5   **End Rhy. Fig. 1**

slight P.M. ---------

𝄋 Verse

1st & 2nd times, w/ Rhy. Fig. 1 (3 3/4 times)
3rd time, tacet (next 15 meas.)

E5	G#5	C#5	A5	C5	D5	B5	D5

1., 3. I'm so | happy 'cause today | I've found my friends, | they're in my head.
2. I'm so | lonely, that's okay, | I shaved my head, | and I'm not sad.

E5	G#5	C#5	A5	C5	D5	B5	D5

I'm so | ugly, that's okay | 'cause so are you, | broke our mirrors.
And just | maybe I'm to blame | for all I've heard, | but I'm not sure.

E5	G#5	C#5	A5	C5	D5	B5	D5

Sunday | morning is ev'ry day | for all I care, | and I'm not scared.
I'm so ex- | cited I can't wait | to meet you there, | but I don't care.

E5	G#5	C#5	A5	C5	D5

Light my | candles in a daze | 'cause I've found God.
I'm so | horny, that's okay, | my will is good.

Pre-Chorus

Yeah,   yeah.   Yeah.   yeah.

B5   D5   E5   G#5   C#5   A5

Rhy. Fig. 2

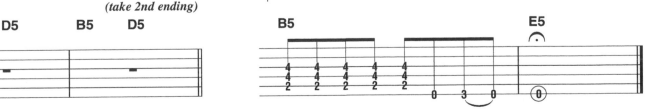

Rebel 'Rouser

By Duane Eddy and Lee Hazlewood

Key of E

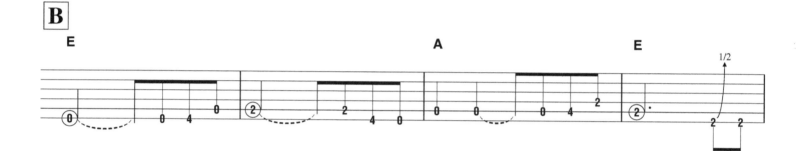

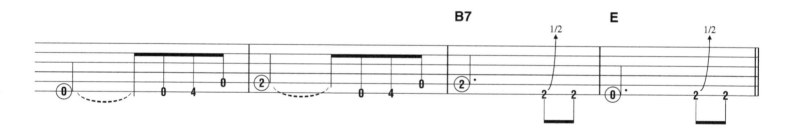

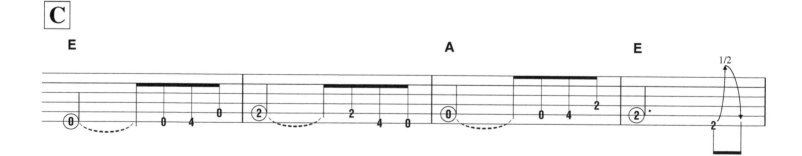

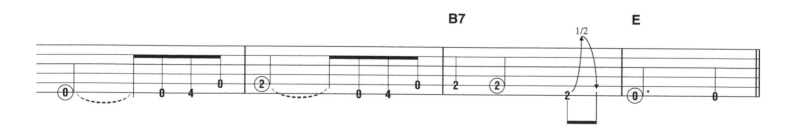

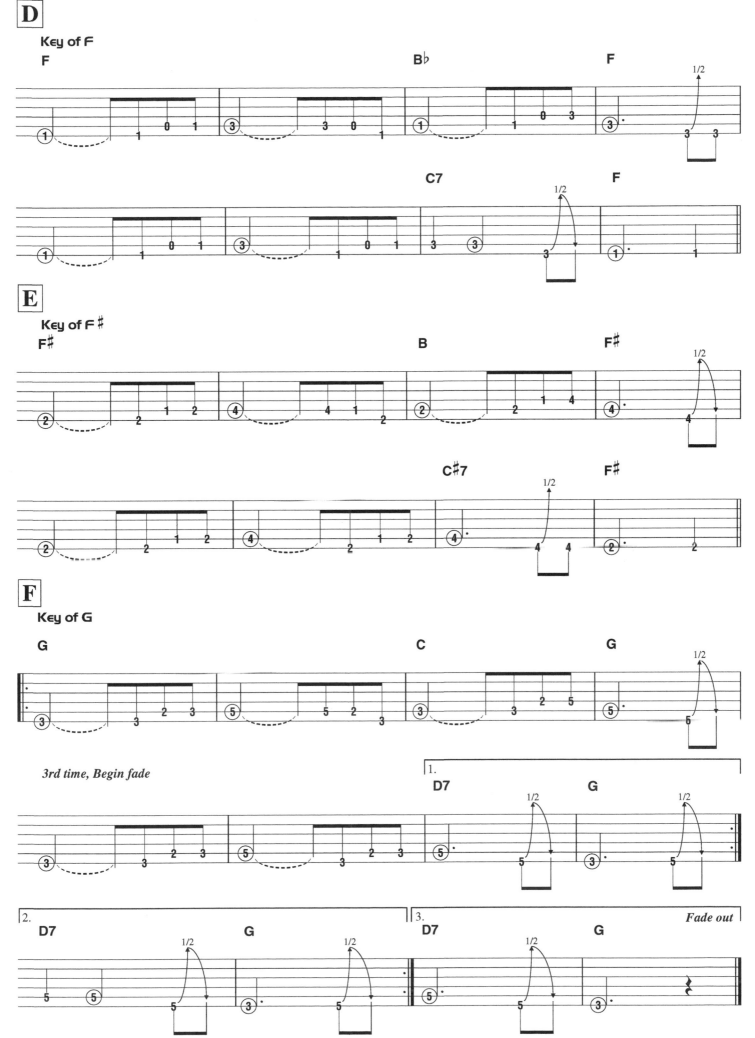

Rolling in the Deep

Words and Music by Adele Adkins and Paul Epworth

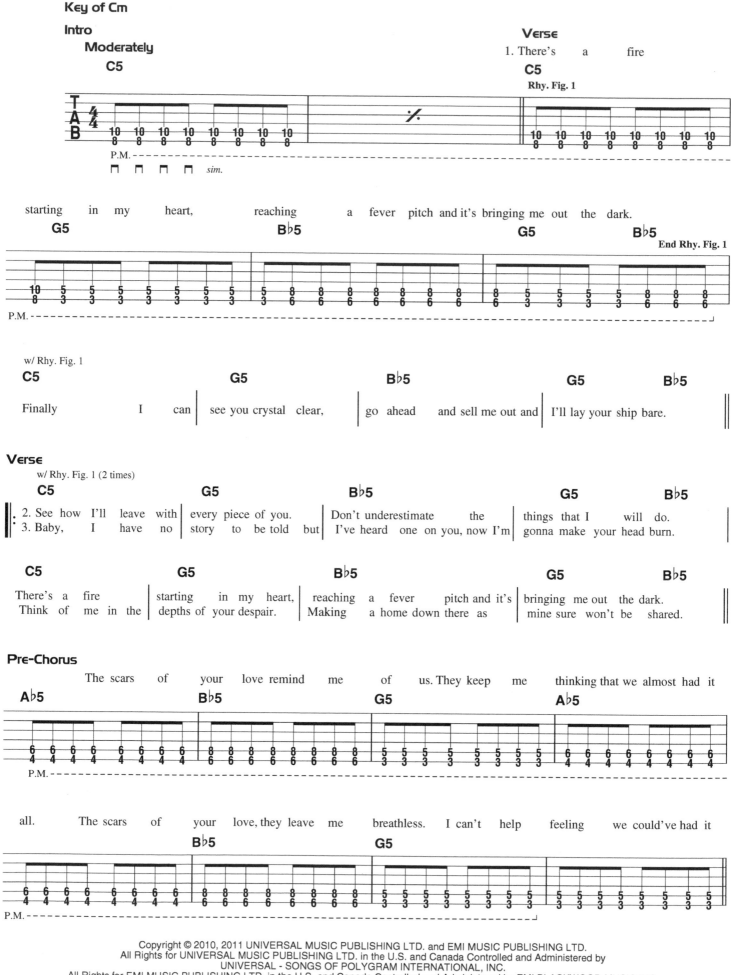

𝄋 Chorus

all.
(You're gonna wish you never had met me. Rolling in the deep. Tears are gonna fall, You had my heart in - rolling in the deep.

C5 — Rhy. Fig. 2   **B♭5**   **A♭5**   **B♭5** — End Rhy. Fig. 2

3rd time, To Coda ⊕

w/ Rhy. Fig. 2
C5   **B♭5**   **A♭5**   **B♭5**

side of your hand, and you played it to the beat. (2., 3.) We could've had it
You're gonna wish you never had met me. Tears are gonna fall, rolling in the deep.

all. Rolling in the deep. You had my heart in -
A♭5   **B♭5**   **C5**   **B♭5**

side of your hand but you played it with a beat - ing.
A♭5   **B♭5**

Verse

Gtr. tacet
N.C.

4. Throw your soul through every open door. Count your blessings to find what you look for.
Turn my sorrow into treasured gold. You'll pay me back in kind and reap just what you sow.

Chorus

C5   **B♭5**   **A♭5**   **B♭5**

(You're gonna wish you never had met me. We could've had it all. Tears are gonna fall, We could've had it rolling in the deep.

D.S. al Coda

C5   **B♭5**   **A♭5**   **B♭5**

all, it all, it all, it all. We could've had it
You're gonna wish you never had met me Tears are gonna fall, rolling in the deep.)

⊕ Coda

w/ Rhy. Fig. 2 (1 1/2 times)
C5   **B♭5**   **A♭5**

all. Rolling in the deep.
You're gonna wish you never had met me. Tears are gonna fall,

B♭5   **C5**   **B♭5**

You had my heart in - side of your hand, but you played
rolling in the deep. You're gonna wish you never had met me.)

it, you played it, you played it, you played it to the beat.
A♭5   **B♭5**   **C5** **N.C.**

Use Somebody

Words and Music by Caleb Followill, Nathan Followill, Jared Followill and Matthew Followill

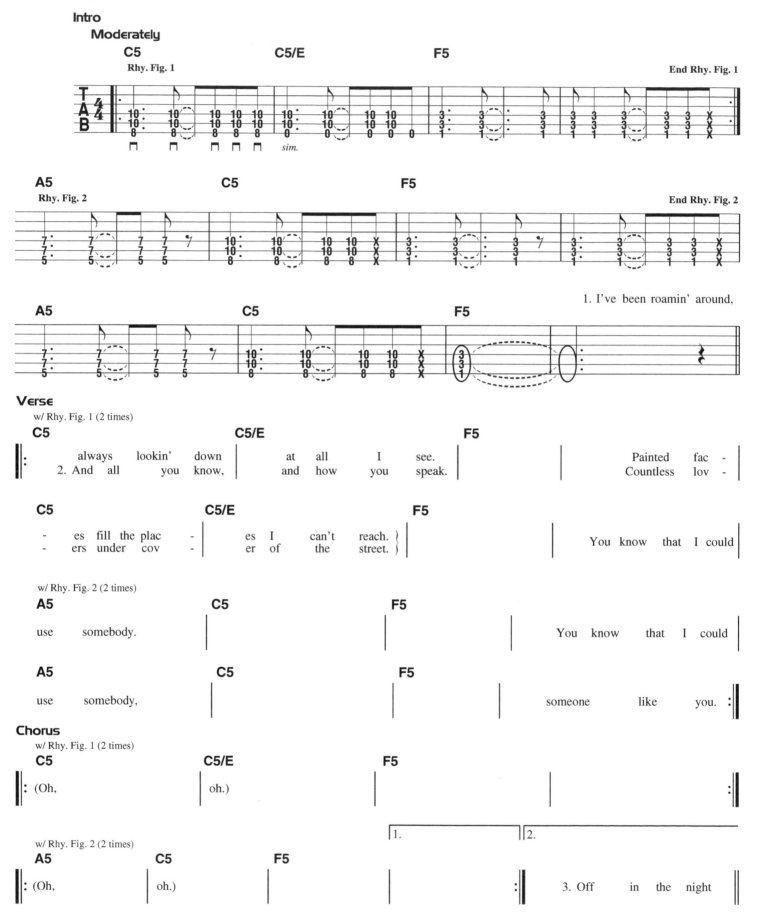

Verse

Gtr. tacet

(C5) ... **(C5/E)** ... **(F5)**

while you live it up,   I'm off to sleep.   Wagin' wars

(C5) ... **(C5/E)** ... **(F5)**

to shake the po - et and the beat.   I hope it's gonna

w/ Rhy. Fig. 2 (2 times)

A5   **C5**   **F5**

1.

2.

make you notice,   I hope it's gonna   someone like me.

Chorus

w/ Rhy. Fig. 1 (2 times)

1.

2.

C5   **C5/E**   **F5**

(Oh,   oh.)   Someone like me.   Someone like me,

w/ Rhy. Fig. 2 (2 times)

A5   **C5**   **F5**   **A5**   **C5**   **F5**

somebody.   (Oh,   oh.)   (Oh,

Bridge
Key of D

1.

2.

let it out. Oh, let it out. Oh, let it out. Oh, let it out Oh, let it out.)

D5   **F♯5**   **B5 N.C.**

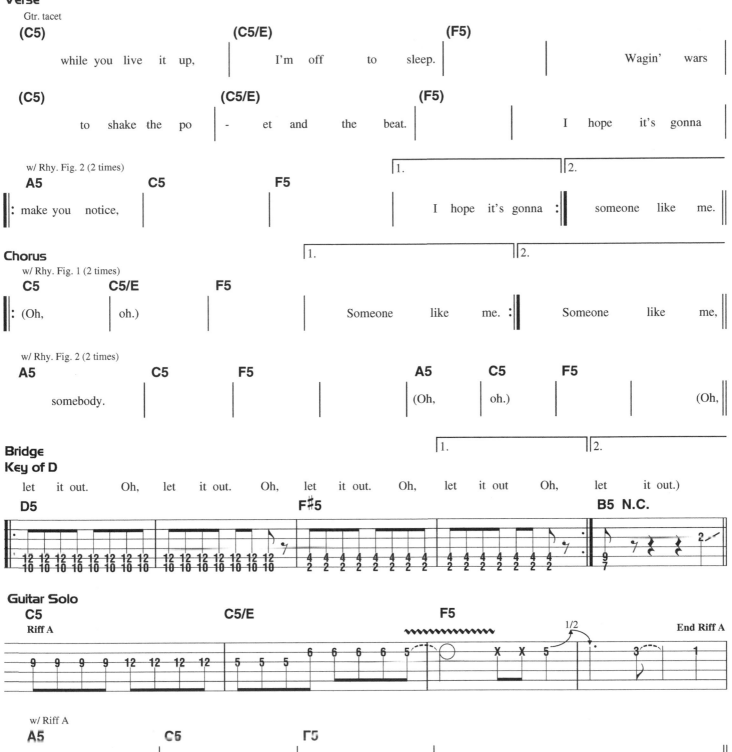

Guitar Solo

C5   **C5/E**   **F5**

Riff A   1/2   End Riff A

w/ Riff A

A5   **C5**   **F5**

Someone like you,

Chorus

w/ Riff A (2 1/4 times)

A5   **C5**   **F5**   **A5**

somebody.   Someone like you,   somebody.

Outro

I've been roamin' around,   always lookin' down   at all I see.

C5   **F5**   **C5**   **C5/E**   **F5**

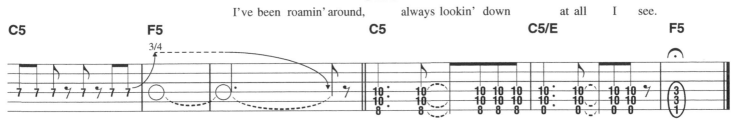

The Zoo

Words and Music by Rudolf Schenker and Klaus Meine

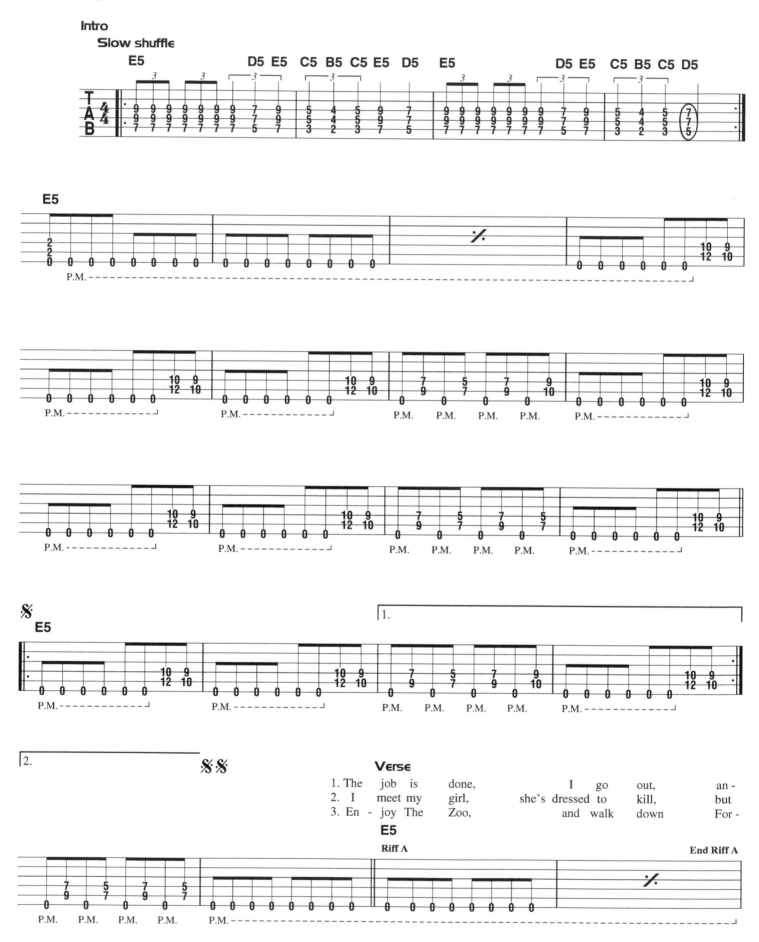

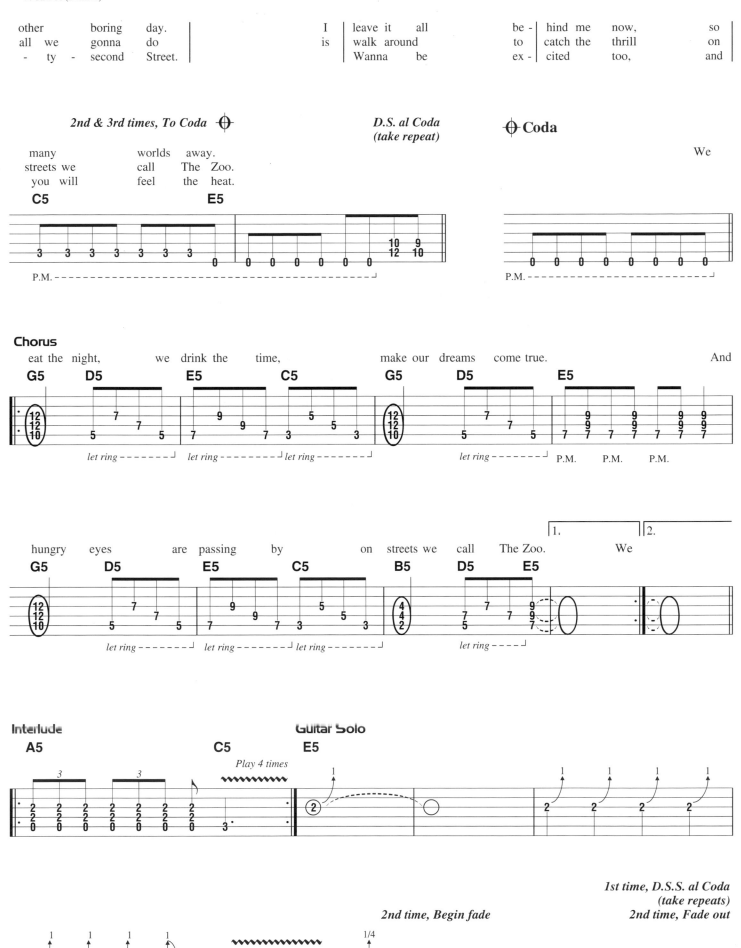

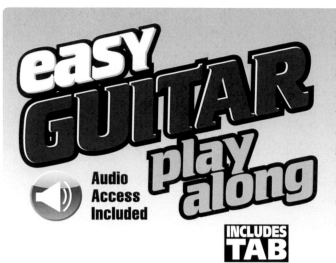

easy GUITAR play along

Audio Access Included

INCLUDES TAB

The *Easy Guitar Play Along*® series features streamlined transcriptions of your favorite songs. Just follow the tab, listen to the audio to hear how the guitar should sound, and then play along using the backing tracks. Playback tools are provided for slowing down the tempo without changing pitch and looping challenging parts. The melody and lyrics are included in the book so that you can sing or simply follow along.

1. ROCK CLASSICS
Jailbreak • Living After Midnight • Mississippi Queen • Rocks Off • Runnin' Down a Dream • Smoke on the Water • Strutter • Up Around the Bend.
00702560 Book/CD Pack....... $14.99

2. ACOUSTIC TOP HITS
About a Girl • I'm Yours • The Lazy Song • The Scientist • 21 Guns • Upside Down • What I Got • Wonderwall.
00702569 Book/CD Pack....... $14.99

3. ROCK HITS
All the Small Things • Best of You • Brain Stew (The Godzilla Remix) • Californication • Island in the Sun • Plush • Smells Like Teen Spirit • Use Somebody.
00702570 Book/CD Pack....... $14.99

4. ROCK 'N' ROLL
Blue Suede Shoes • I Get Around • I'm a Believer • Jailhouse Rock • Oh, Pretty Woman • Peggy Sue • Runaway • Wake Up Little Susie.
00702572 Book/CD Pack....... $14.99

6. CHRISTMAS SONGS
Have Yourself a Merry Little Christmas • A Holly Jolly Christmas • The Little Drummer Boy • Run Rudolph Run • Santa Claus Is Comin' to Town • Silver and Gold • Sleigh Ride • Winter Wonderland.
00101879 Book/CD Pack........ $14.99

7. BLUES SONGS FOR BEGINNERS
Come On (Part 1) • Double Trouble • Gangster of Love • I'm Ready • Let Me Love You Baby • Mary Had a Little Lamb • San-Ho-Zay • T-Bone Shuffle.
00103235 Book/
    Online Audio..........$17.99

9. ROCK SONGS FOR BEGINNERS
Are You Gonna Be My Girl • Buddy Holly • Everybody Hurts • In Bloom • Otherside • The Rock Show • Santa Monica • When I Come Around.
00103255 Book/CD Pack.....$14.99

10. GREEN DAY
Basket Case • Boulevard of Broken Dreams • Good Riddance (Time of Your Life) • Holiday • Longview • 21 Guns • Wake Me up When September Ends • When I Come Around.
00122322 Book/
    Online Audio $16.99

11. NIRVANA
All Apologies • Come As You Are • Heart Shaped Box • Lake of Fire • Lithium • The Man Who Sold the World • Rape Me • Smells Like Teen Spirit.
00122325 Book/
    Online Audio $17.99

13. AC/DC
Back in Black • Dirty Deeds Done Dirt Cheap • For Those About to Rock (We Salute You) • Hells Bells • Highway to Hell • Rock and Roll Ain't Noise Pollution • T.N.T. • You Shook Me All Night Long.
14042895 Book/
    Online Audio........ $17.99

14. JIMI HENDRIX – SMASH HITS
All Along the Watchtower • Can You See Me • Crosstown Traffic • Fire • Foxey Lady • Hey Joe • Manic Depression • Purple Haze • Red House • Remember • Stone Free • The Wind Cries Mary.
00130591 Book/
    Online Audio........$24.99

HAL•LEONARD®
www.halleonard.com

Prices, contents, and availability subject to change without notice.